P9-ELU-781
DINOSHARKS!

DINOSHARKS!

Written by Jodell Sadler and
Professor John A. Long, Strategic Professor in Paleontology
Research Section Head, Ecology and Evolution
Flinders University, Australia

Illustrated by Simon Mendez

Designed by Mickey Gill Creative

10 9 8 7 6 5 4 3 2 1

ISBN: 978-1-338-54101-4

Created in the USA
Printed in Jiaxing, China

The information and renderings in this book are true and complete to the best of our knowledge and research available.

CONTENTS

A LONG TIME AGO IN THE DEEP BLUE SEA

Dinosaurs may win the popularity contest when it comes to famous **extinct** reptiles, but long before dinosaurs roamed the earth, **prehistoric** sharks dominated its oceans. For more than 400 million years, massive oceanic beasts lived deep within the waters, stalking and ripping apart prey such as dinosaurs, whales, and even each other!

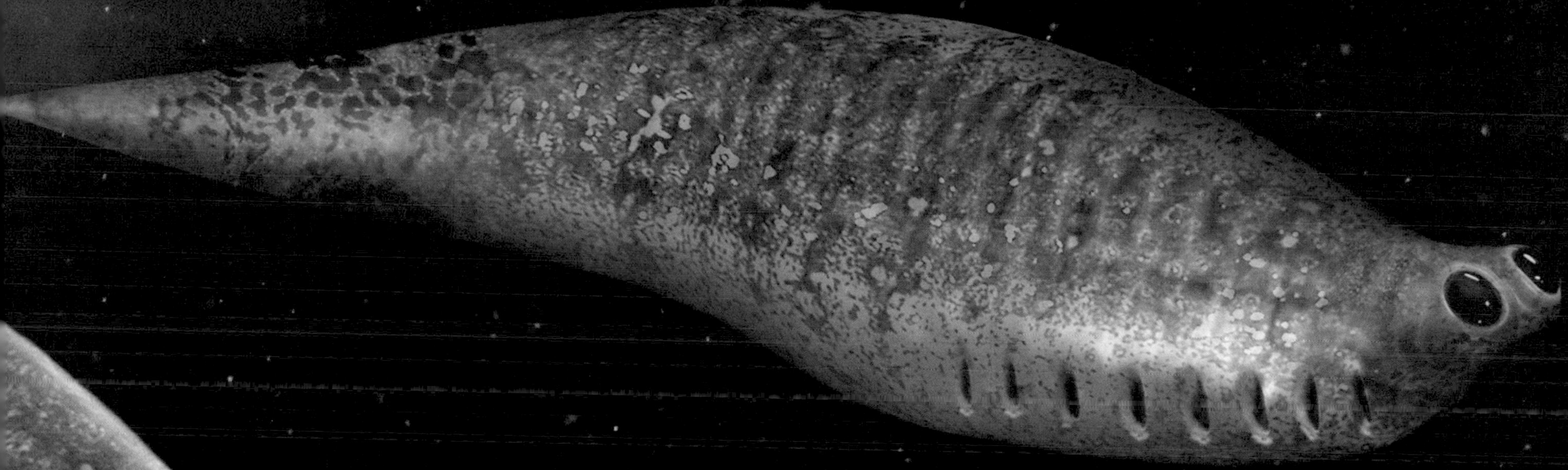

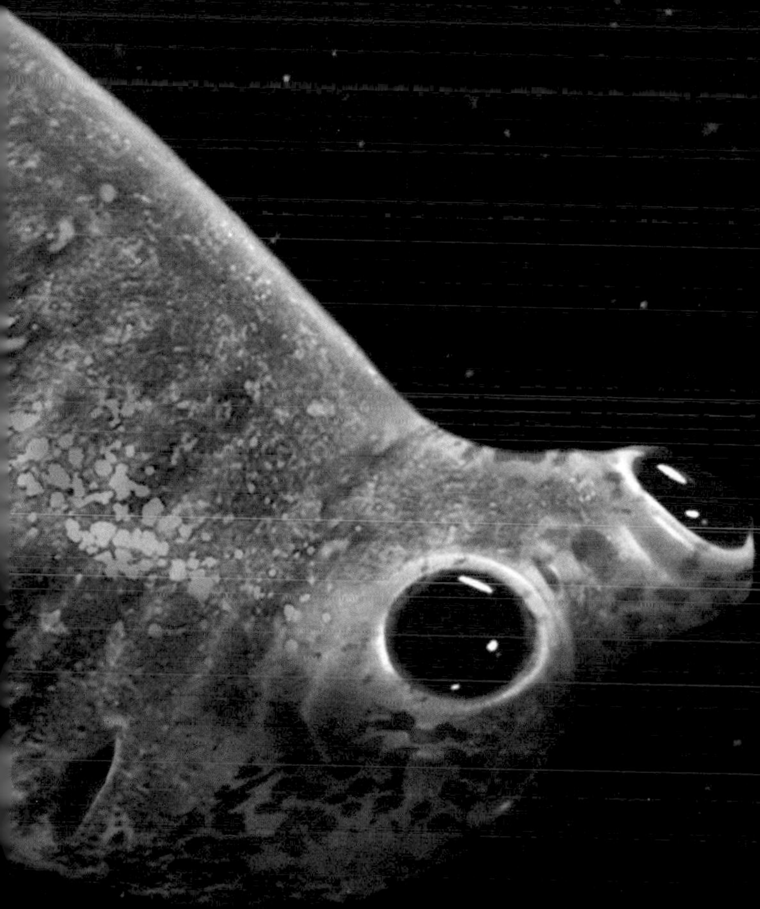

WHERE IT ALL BEGAN

Metaspriggina, a tiny wormlike **fossil** fish that lived between 513 to 501 million years ago, is the original ancestor of prehistoric sharks, and the oldest fish ever found!

As members of the fish family, prehistoric and modern sharks have unique qualities that make them stand out from the tuna and salmon of today. Instead of bone, sharks have lightweight **cartilage**. They also have multiple gill slits, teeth that grow back, and a rough sandpaper-like skin.

FIRST REAL SHARK:

LEONODUS

LEE-ON-OH-DUSS

Scientists believe the first sharks appeared about 460 million years ago. They know this from studying layers and layers of sand and clay that hardened to form **sedimentary** rock. Sedimentary rock preserves plants and the bones of animals, resulting in fossils. Scientists found the ancient two-pronged teeth of this shark in sedimentary rocks. They dated the rocks from radiometric decay of minerals to get its precise age. *Leonodus* was only about a foot (30.5 cm) long but its sharp teeth tell us it likely fed on other fish.

A handful of tiny scales are the only evidence of the earliest sharks.
Triassic
Jurassic
Cretaceous
Paleogene
Neogene
-251
-201
-145
-66
-23
-2

SMALL BUT MIGHTY SHARK:

CTENACANTHUS

TEEN-AH-CAN-THUSS

Ctenacanthus was a ferocious 5 foot (1.5 m) long **predator** that ate smaller fish and other sharks. Each of its teeth had many sharp **cusps** for catching its prey and trapping prey inside its large mouth. The two deadly spines protected it from being swallowed by the terrifying *Dunkleosteus,* which grew to 25 feet (7.6 m) in length.

Length: 5 feet (1.5 m)
Weight: Unknown
Prey: Unknown
Found in: United States, Europe, and South America

Silurian | Devonian | Carboniferous | Permian

-443 | -419 | -359 | -298 | -25

MILLIONS OF YEARS

Sharks are fish! The study of prehistoric fish is called paleoichthyology.
Triassic
Jurassic
Cretaceous
Paleogene
Neogene
51
-201
-145
-66
-23
-2

FIRST MODERN-LOOKING SHARK:

CLADOSELACHE

CLAY-DO-SELL-AH-KEE

Cladoselache was a sleek shark with many rows of teeth showing sharp, pointed fangs. The remains of its last meals have been found in fossils. Some were cannibals, eating their own species! *Cladoselache* was a fast swimmer, as shown by its slender shape and large tail fin. Unlike modern sharks with mouths on the bottom of their heads, *Cladoselache's* mouth was up front. It also had very few scales.

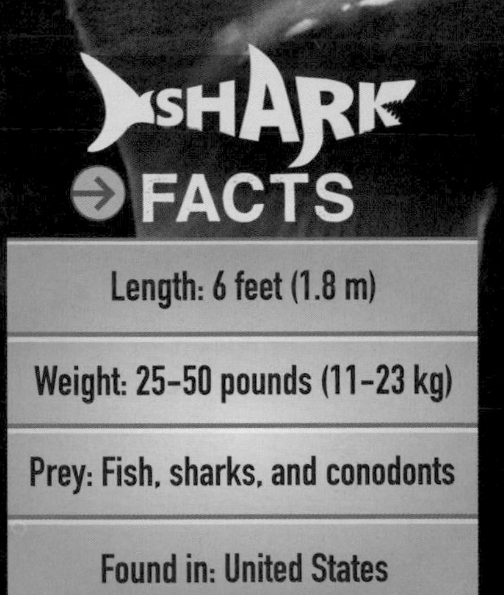

Length: 6 feet (1.8 m)
Weight: 25–50 pounds (11–23 kg)
Prey: Fish, sharks, and conodonts
Found in: United States

Silurian | Devonian | Carboniferous | Permian

-443 -419 -359 -298 -25

MILLIONS OF YEARS

Scientists believe the *Cladoselache* grabbed its prey by the tail and swallowed it whole!
Triassic
Jurassic
Cretaceous
Paleogene
Neogene
251
-201
-145
-66
-23
-2

AMAZING EEL-LIKE SHARK:

XENACANTHUS

ZEE-NAH-CAN-THUS

Xenacanthus lived in both seas and rivers. Its long, slender body sported a long razor-sharp spike on its neck. This spike was not venomous like that of the modern stingray, but it served to protect the shark from attacks by much larger killer fish like the 20 foot (6.1 m) long *Rhizodus.*

Length: 3 feet (1.8 m)
Weight: Up to 30 pounds (13.6 kg)
Prey: Fish, other sharks, crustaceans, and possibly early amphibians
Found in: United States, Europe, and India

Silurian | Devonian | Carboniferous | Permian

-443 | -419 | -359 | -298 | -25

MILLIONS OF YEARS

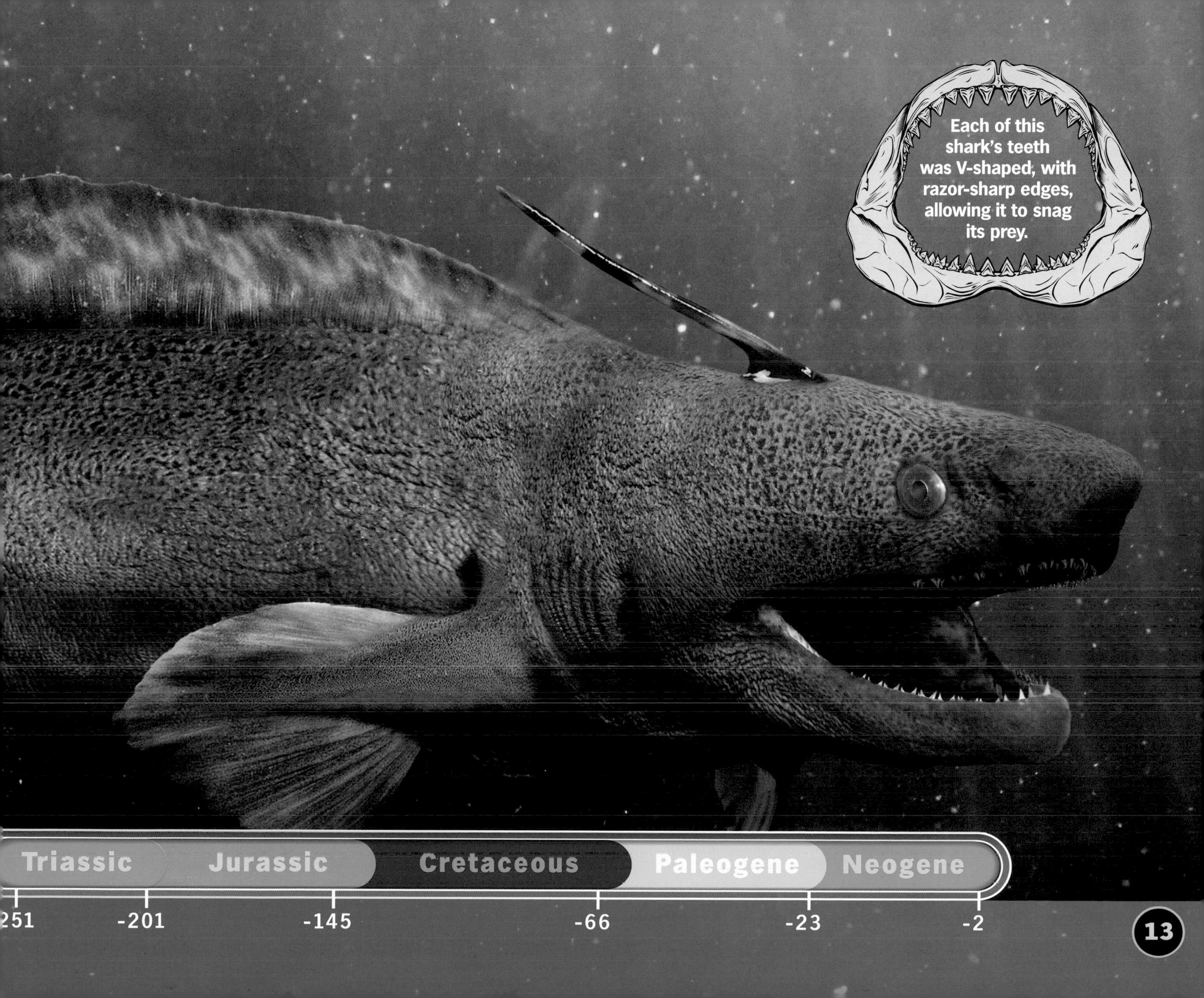
Each of this shark's teeth was V-shaped, with razor-sharp edges, allowing it to snag its prey.
Triassic
Jurassic
Cretaceous
Paleogene
Neogene
-251
-201
-145
-66
-23
-2

WEIRDEST-LOOKING ANCIENT SHARK:

STETHACANTHUS

STETH-AH-CAN-THUSS

The strange-looking *Stethacanthus* had a clever trick for protecting itself from being eaten. Its **dorsal fin** had a thick, bony brush full of teeth-like spines, as did the top of its head. This might have scared away larger fish from eating it, as it resembled an open mouth full of teeth. Its super-long **pectoral fins** had long, slender whips that helped when the fish were mating.

Length: 2 feet (0.7 m)

Weight: 10 pounds (4.5 kg)

Prey: Fish, crustaceans, and worms

Found: Worldwide

Silurian | Devonian | Carboniferous | Permian

-443 | -419 | -359 | -298 | -251

MILLIONS OF YEARS

Each tooth on the dorsal fin was made of one large curved fang. Each tooth inside the mouth had many small fangs.
Triassic
Jurassic
Cretaceous
Paleogene
Neogene
251
-201
-145
-66
-23
-2

SMALL, BIG-EYED SHARK:

FALCATUS

FAL-KATE-US

Falcatus males had a long, curved spine in front of the dorsal fin that extended above the head to attract females. They hunted in shallow, warm seas close to the land, eating shrimp and smaller fish. Their large eyes suggest they hunted their prey mostly at night.

Length: 1 foot (0.3 m)
Weight: 1 pound (0.45 kg)
Prey: Shrimp and other small invertebrates
Found in: United States

Silurian | Devonian | Carboniferous | Permian

-443 | -419 | -359 | -298 | -251

MILLIONS OF YEARS

No bones about it—sharks' skeletons are made of cartilage, not bones!
Triassic
Jurassic
Cretaceous
Paleogene
Neogene
51
-201
-145
-66
-23
-2

SHARK FACTS
Length: 20 feet (6 m)
Weight: 500 pounds (225 kg)
Prey: Jellyfish, clams, and shellfish
Found in: England, Russia, and United States
Silurian
Devonian
Carboniferous
Permian
-443
-419
-359
-298
-25
MILLIONS OF YEARS

SCARY, SCISSOR-TOOTHED SHARK:

ED-DESS-TUSS

Sharks today lose their teeth constantly, but not this prehistoric predator! Instead of its teeth falling out, its teeth grew one behind the other, pushing the older teeth forward and creating rows of really sharp—and really big—teeth! No wonder its nickname is the scissor-toothed shark!

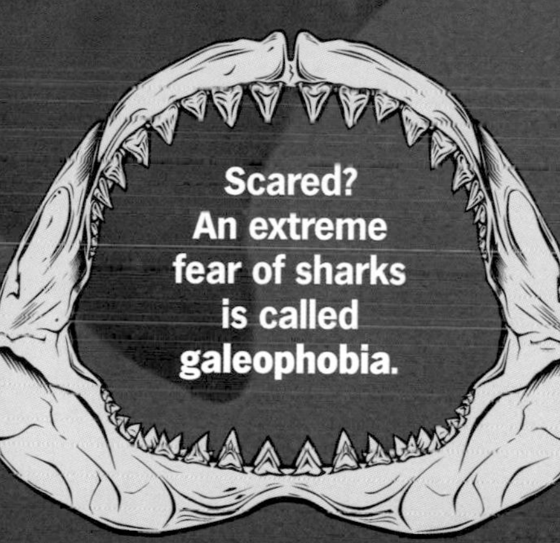

Scared? An extreme fear of sharks is called galeophobia.

Triassic | Jurassic | Cretaceous | Paleogene | Neogene

51 | -201 | -145 | -66 | -23 | -2

SPOONBILL-SNOUTED SHARK:

BANDRINGA

BAN-DRING-AH

Bandringa had a long snout with special **electroreceptor** cells to detect its prey, even when the prey is hidden in soft sand on the seafloor. It fed on small crabs and clams, which it could dig out using its spoon-shaped snout. *Bandringa* had tiny teeth, perfect for its seafood diet!

- Length: 10 feet (3 m)
- Weight: Unknown
- Prey: Worms, shrimp, and small aquatic animals
- Found in: United States

Silurian | Devonian | Carboniferous | Permian

-443 | -419 | -359 | -298 | -25

MILLIONS OF YEARS

The female *Bandringa* swam from fresh water to salt water to lay her eggs, a rare behavior.
Triassic
Jurassic
Cretaceous
Paleogene
Neogene
51
-201
-145
-66
-23
-2

SMALL, BULGY-HEADED SHARK:

COBELODUS

CO-BE-LO-DUS

Cobelodus was a fast-moving, active predator that had a bulging head, an arched back, and a single large dorsal fin near its tail. It also had two unusual foot-long (.3-m) whips extending from its pectoral fin. Its razor-sharp teeth had many daggerlike blades on each tooth, perfect to catch and slice up the small fish it loved to eat.

Length: 7 feet (2 m)
Weight: Unknown
Prey: Fish and squid-like animals
Found in: United States

Silurian | Devonian | Carboniferous | Permian

-443 | -419 | -359 | -298 | -25

MILLIONS OF YEARS

Some sharks drown if they stop moving, but others can pump water over their gills to get oxygen even if they take a nap.

Triassic | Jurassic | Cretaceous | Paleogene | Neogene

51 -201 -145 -66 -23 -2

ODD, ANCIENT 'BUZZSAW' SHARK:

HELICOPRION

HEL-E-CO-PREE-ON

Helicoprion was the world's first megapredator, reaching up to 25 feet (7.62 m) long. It had a unique **tooth whorl** on its lower jaw made up of a spiral of 300 razor-sharp **serrated** teeth. Its upper jaw was toothless. It may have fed by charging into schools of fish and squid to wound prey and then coming back to gobble up the bleeding prey.

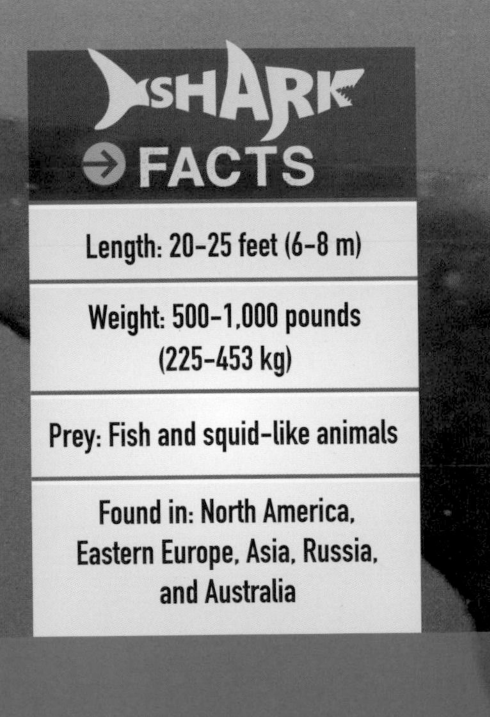

Silurian | Devonian | Carboniferous | Permian

-443 | -419 | -359 | -298 | -25

MILLIONS OF YEARS

The *Helicoprion* survived "The Great Dying," a mass extinction that took place 250 million years ago.
Triassic
Jurassic
Cretaceous
Paleogene
Neogene
251
-201
-145
-66
-23
-2

HUMPED-TOOTH THRESHER SHARK:

HYBODUS

HIGH-BO-DUSS

Hybodus lived from the Permian to Cretaceous periods. It was a specialist when it came to feeding, and it was the first shark to have very different kinds of teeth in its mouth. It had sharp, piercing teeth up front for grabbing prey, and flat pavement teeth for crushing its food at the back of its mouth. An extended tail lobe helped it cruise slowly along while searching the riverbeds for its prey.

Length: 6 feet (2 m)
Weight: 200 pounds (90 kg)
Prey: Fish, crustaceans, clams, and squid-like animals
Found: Worldwide

Silurian | Devonian | Carboniferous | Permian

-443 | -419 | -359 | -298 | -251

MILLIONS OF YEARS

For sharks, there is no gray area. They only see in black and white.
Triassic
Jurassic
Cretaceous
Paleogene
Neogene
251
-201
-145
-66
-23
-2

BIG BLUNTNOSE SIXGILL SHARK:

HEXANCHUS

HEX-AN-CHUS

This ancient creature, which lived with the dinosaurs, still roams our ocean waters today! One of the oldest creatures on Earth, three species of the *Hexanchus* still exist: Bluntnose, Bigeyed, and Atlantic Sixgills. They have wide, pointed heads, six pairs of gill slits, and long tails. But they are easy to miss. They are **nocturnal** and stay in waters as deep as 2,500 feet (760 m)!

Length: 16–26 feet (5–8 m)
Weight: 1,300 pounds (590 kg)
Prey: Sharks, rays, chimaeras, bony fish, squid, shellfish, and seals
Found: Worldwide

Silurian | Devonian | Carboniferous | Permian

-443 | -419 | -359 | -298 | -25

MILLIONS OF YEARS

The female swam to warm, shallow waters and gave birth to a litter of 22 to 100 live pups!
Triassic
Jurassic
Cretaceous
Paleogene
Neogene
251
-201
-145
-66
-23
-2

LONG, FLAT-NOSED GOBLIN SHARK:

SCAPANORHYNCHUS

SCAP-AN-O-RINK-US

Scapanorhynchus prowled the deep waters during the reign of *Tyrannosaurus rex*. Its long, flat snout held electroreceptors that detected prey at the darkest, murkiest depths. *Scapanorhynchus*, which has relatives that are still alive today, didn't need light or sight to catch a squid!

Length: 11 feet (3 m)

Weight: 460 pounds (210 kg)

Prey: Fish, shrimp, and squid

Found: Worldwide

Silurian | Devonian | Carboniferous | Permian

-443 | -419 | -359 | -298 | -251

MILLIONS OF YEARS

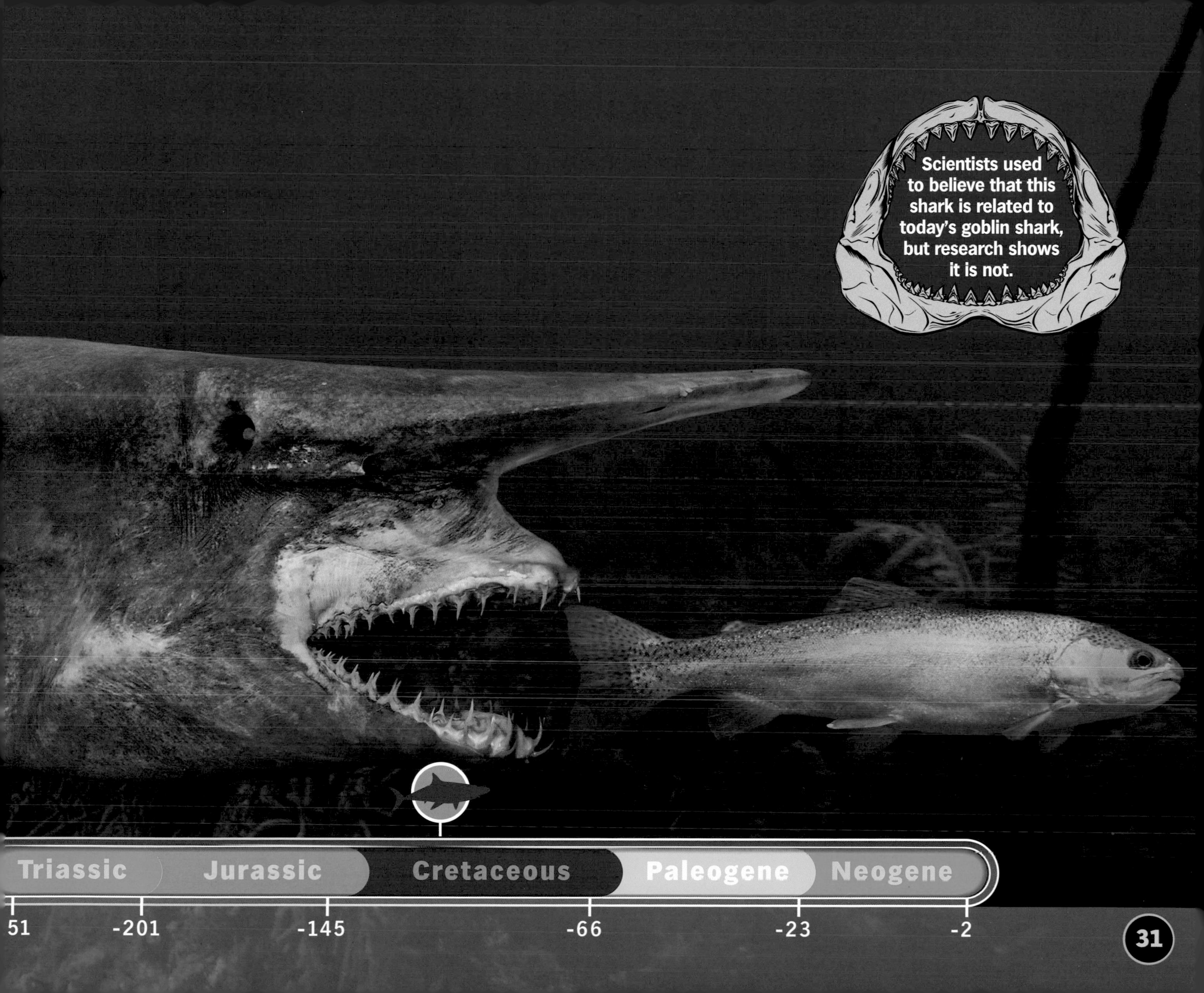
Scientists used to believe that this shark is related to today's goblin shark, but research shows it is not.
Triassic
Jurassic
Cretaceous
Paleogene
Neogene
51
-201
-145
-66
-23
-2

FIERCE-BITING CROW SHARK:

SQUALICORAX

SKWA-LIH-CORE-AX

Squalicorax was a large coastal predator that ate almost anything it could find, even dinosaurs! It had stout, serrated teeth like a tiger shark. It ate turtles, mosasaurs, and even pterosaurs. One *Squalicorax* tooth was found stuck in a duck-billed dinosaur's tailbone, indicating this shark scavenged on dinosaur carcasses swept out to sea by floods.

Length: 6-16 feet (1.9-5 m)

Weight: 500-1000 pounds (227-454 kg)

Prey: Fish, turtles, mosasaurs, peterosaurs, and dinosaur carcasses

Found in: North America, Europe, and North Africa

Silurian | Devonian | Carboniferous | Permian

-443 | -419 | -359 | -298 | -25

MILLIONS OF YEARS

Squalicorax was an expert scavenger of dead carcasses.
Triassic
Jurassic
Cretaceous
Paleogene
Neogene
251
-201
-145
-66
-23
-2

Length: 25 feet (6.7 m)

Weight: 1,000–2,000 pounds (454–907 kg)

Prey: Bony fish, mosasaurs, and plesiosaurs

Found: Worldwide

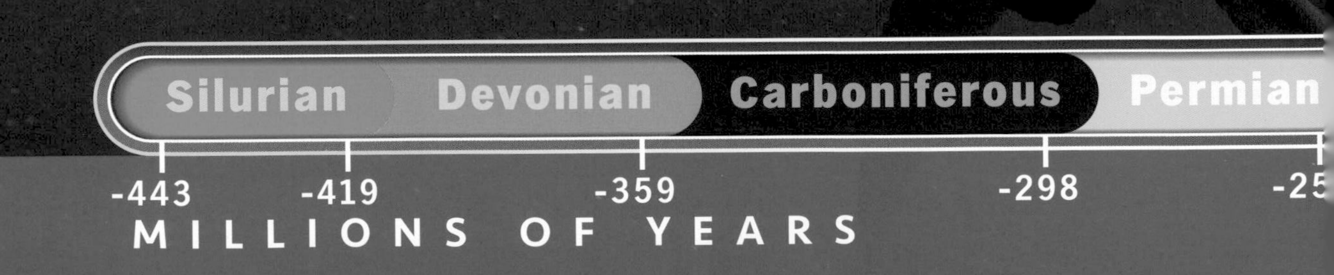

SHARP-CUTTING 'GINSU' SHARK:

CRETOXYRHINA

CREH-TOX-EE-RYE-NAH

Nicknamed the "Ginsu" shark for its mouth full of bone-slicing teeth, the ferocious *Cretoxyrhina* attacked its prey and sliced through bones of plesiosaurs and mosasaurs like butter. It was the largest killer shark of the dinosaur era.

Every year, fewer than five people are killed by sharks, but more than 100 million sharks are killed by humans.

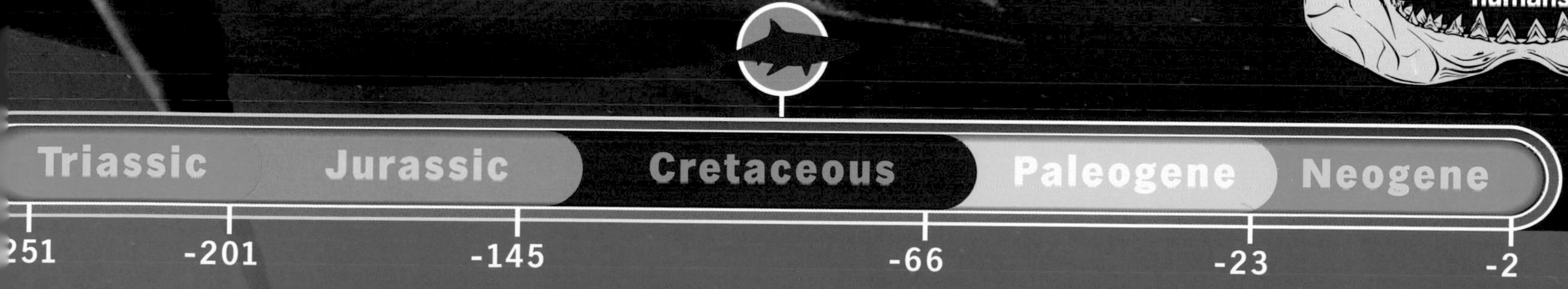

Triassic | Jurassic | Cretaceous | Paleogene | Neogene

-251 | -201 | -145 | -66 | -23 | -2

HIGHLY SPECIALIZED ODDBALL SHARK:

PTYCHODUS

TIE-COE-DUS

Ptychodus was a monster shark more than 33 feet (10 m) long, with large, crinkled, dome-shaped teeth for crushing giant clams about 3 feet (1 m) wide, which formed reefs on the bottom of the ocean at the time *Ptychodus* lived.

Length: 32 feet (10 m)

Weight: 1000–2000 pounds (453–907 kg)

Prey: Shellfish and crustaceans

Found in: Europe, Canada, United States, and Australia

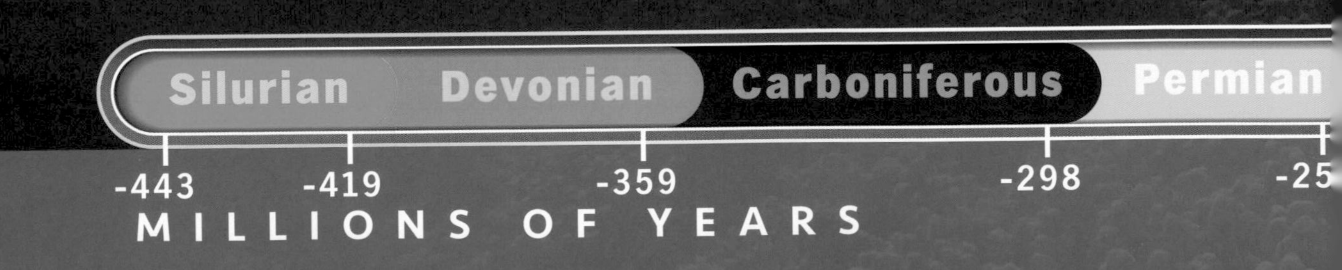

Ptychodus most likely fed on *Inoceramus*, the largest clams to have ever lived.
Triassic
Jurassic
Cretaceous
Paleogene
Neogene
51
-201
-145
-66
-23
-2

FLESH-RIPPING GIANT SHARK:

OTODUS

OH-TOE-DUS

Otodus was a fierce, flesh-ripping giant shark with razor-sharp teeth that eventually developed serrations on them. They fed on sharks, whales, and large fish. New fossil evidence suggests this shark was the ancestor to the *Carcharocles* family of sharks, which includes megalodon.

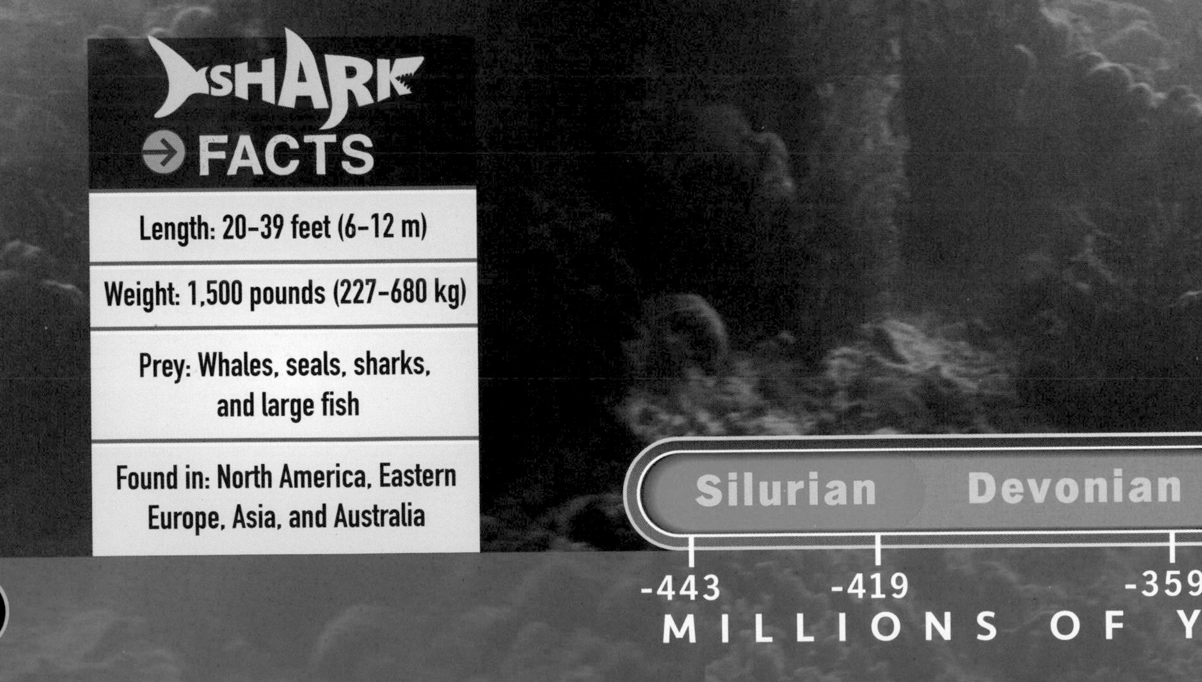

SHARK FACTS

Length: 20–39 feet (6–12 m)
Weight: 1,500 pounds (227–680 kg)
Prey: Whales, seals, sharks, and large fish
Found in: North America, Eastern Europe, Asia, and Australia

Otodus was nearly twice the size of a great white shark.

LARGEST SHARK SPECIES TO EVER LIVE:

MEGALODON

MEG-AH-LOW-DON

Meet the mighty megalodon! Its name means "big tooth," and it's easy to understand why. The largest megalodon tooth measured 7 inches (17.8 cm) long. With five rows of these thick, serrated teeth, this marine monster could rip apart humpbacks, giant squid, and even a 50-foot (15.2-m) prehistoric whale called the *Livyatan!*

Length: 33–39 feet (15–17 m)
Weight: 60–100 tons (54–90 m tons)
Prey: Whales, large fish, and giant squid
Found: Worldwide

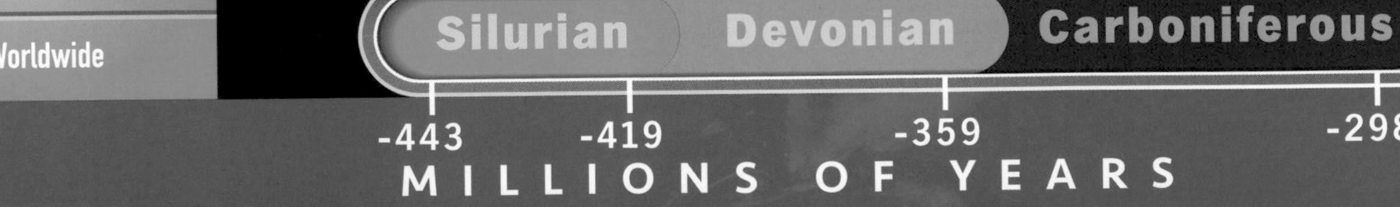

The Ice Age killed more than 80 percent of shark species due to drastic drops in sea level and water temperature.
Triassic
Jurassic
Cretaceous
Paleogene
Neogene
51
-201
-145
-66
-23
-2

THE EVOLUTION OF THE MEGALODON:

FROM CRETACEOUS TO NEOGENE

OTODUS OBLIQUUS

O-TOE-DUS O-BLEEK-US

Paleogene to Neogene period, 66 to 20 million years ago.

Length: 30 feet (9 m) Weight: 1–2 tons (900–1,800 kg)

CARCHAROLES AURICULATUS

KAR-KA-ROE-CLEES OR-REE-CU-LA-TUS

Paleogene to Neogene period, 35 to 25 million years ago.

Length: 30 feet (9 m) Weight: 1–2 tons (900–1,800 kg)

CARCHAROLES ANGUSTIDENS

KAR-KA-ROE-CLEES AN-GUS-TEE-DENZ

Paleogene to Neogene period, 33 to 22 million years ago.

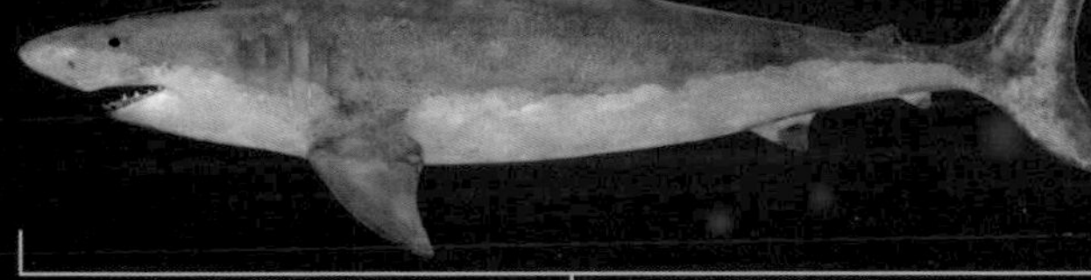

Length: 20 feet (6 m) Weight: 1–2 tons (900–1,800 kg)

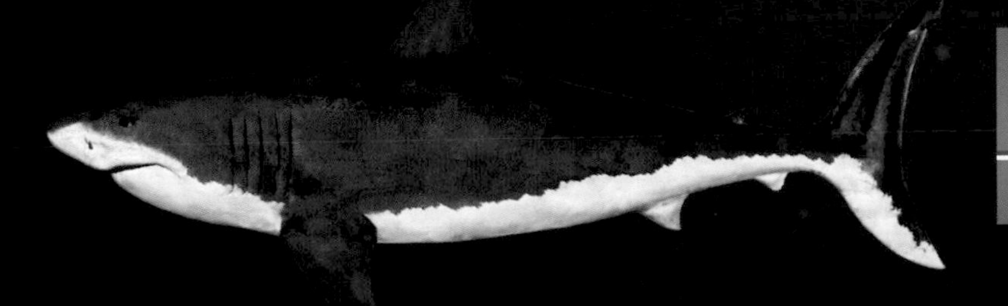

CARCHAROLES CHUBUTENIS

KAR-KA-ROE-CLEES CHU-BU-TEN-SIS

Neogene period, 23 to 3 million years ago.

Length: 13–23 feet (4–7 m) Weight: 1–2 tons (900–1,800 kg)

CARCHAROLES MEGALODON

KAR-KA-ROE-CLEES MEG-AH-LOW-DON

Neogene period, 23 to 2.6 million years ago.

Length: 52 feet (16 m) Weight: 52 tons (47 metric tons)

THE END OF MEGALODON

What could have killed off the most fearsome predator to ever live?

Two words: Ice Age! Around 2.6 million years ago, glaciers grew and polar ice sheets expanded around the globe, making sea levels and their temperatures drop.

This global cooling drove many large warm-blooded whales to feed in the rich Antarctic seas. Megalodon, like all cold-blooded sharks, was not able to tolerate the freezing polar waters, so it couldn't find enough food to survive.

Megalodon had a lot of teeth—about 20,000 during its lifetime. It could grow a new tooth in just two days.

A megalodon's bite was about 30 times stronger than the bite of an African lion. It was even stronger than the mighty *T. rex!*

Scientists believe the average megalodon was about 33 feet (10 m) long, and weighed about 10 times as much as a great white shark.

MEGALODON MODERN MYSTERIES

Some people believe the megalodon still exists! Since its extinction, individuals have caught sightings of beastly sharks lurking in deep waters, even though there is no new fossil evidence that it is alive today.

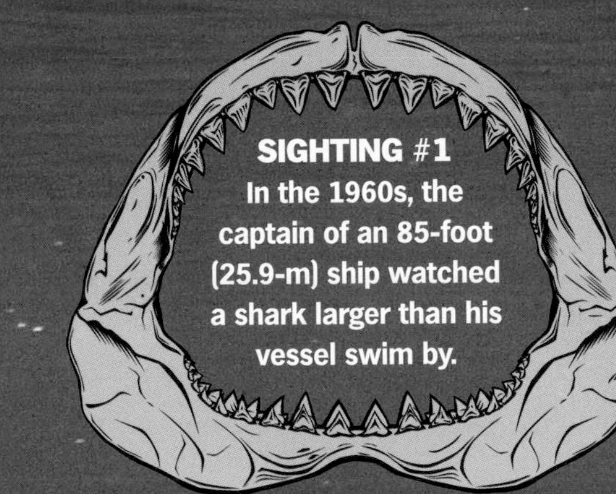

SIGHTING #2
In 2010, an ocean camera placed in South African waters filmed a shark measuring about 62 feet (18.8 m).

SIGHTING #3
In 2017, a NASA satellite photo identified a shark larger than a school bus.

Great white shark sighting
off the coast of Oahu, Hawaii.
January, 2019

Megalodon has gone extinct, and mature sharks—like this grandma great white—are becoming increasingly rare. Help keep sharks around for future generations to enjoy—and help keep the ocean healthy!

GLOSSARY

Cartilage/Cartilaginous – a firm but flexible type of tissue found in sharks, instead of bones

Cusp – pointed end where two curves meet

Dorsal fin – the top fin on the back of a shark

Electroreceptors – a special sensor in sharks that allows them to detect prey

Evidence – facts that are used to prove a belief or **prediction**

Extinct – when an entire species dies out

Fossil – the remains of a living organism (animal, plant, or microbe) preserved in rock, ash, or sedimentary layers

Galeophobia - a fear of sharks

Glacier – slow-flowing river of ice

Global – found around the entire world

Marine – relating to the sea or ocean

New moon – the first phase of the moon, where it can't be seen

Nocturnal – when a living creature feeds at night instead of the daytime

Paleoichthyology – the study of prehistoric fish and fossils

Pectoral fin – pair of fins located on both sides of a shark's head

Petrified – to turn into stone

Predators – a living thing that preys on other living things

Predictions – a statement about what will or may happen in the future

Prehistoric – the time before recorded human history

Sediment – grains of very small rock, like clay, silt, or sand; these can harden over time and become sedimentary rocks

Serrated – having notched or sawlike teeth that point forward

Species – a group of living organisms consisting of similar individuals

Superstitious – a belief that certain events or things will bring good or bad luck

Tooth whorl – teeth arranged in a spiral cluster

Sea and Sky
Around 2,000 years ago, some people believed shark teeth were stones that fell from the sky during a **new moon**.

Tongue and Teeth
Around 500 years ago, some people believed shark teeth were the **petrified** tongues of dragons.